This book belongs to

_____

This book is dedicated to my children - Mikey, Kobe, and Jojo.

Copyright © 2021 by Grow Grit Press LLC. All rights reserved. No part of this book may be reproduced in any form without permission in writing from the publisher. Please send bulk order requests to growgritpress@gmail.com 978-1-63731-121-9 Printed and bound in the USA. MiniMovers.tv

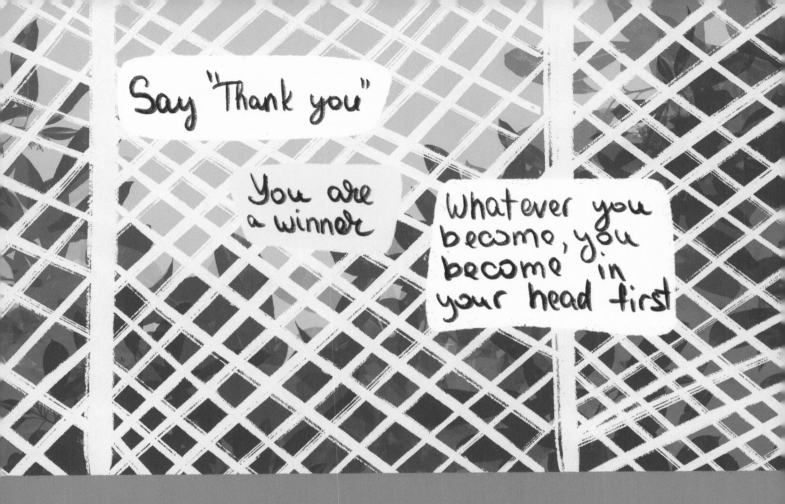

Say "Thank you"

You are a winner

Whatever you become, you become in your head first

By Mary Nhin

Pictures By Yuliia Zolotova

Serena Williams

My dad was watching a tennis match one day. The news reporter announced that a female tennis player had won over $40,000 in one week of tournament play.

My father couldn't believe how much these women were earning just for playing tennis. He thought this might be something good for his daughters. So, he learned the game through books and instructional videos. And whatever he learned, he passed on to us.

Tennis was a way for our family to spend time together. My mother played and so did all four of my older sisters.

I don't remember my first tennis memory because, for me, tennis is like breathing. According to some, I was three years old when my dad first put a racket in my hand. I was tiny and my parents only had money for a regular size racket, not a junior one.

When I got older, around the age of five and Venus was six, we would practice more than once a day.

I liked it because we were all together.
That's what was really important.

When I wasn't playing tennis, one of my favorite pastimes was playing UNO with my family. This game, in particular, really fostered a winning mindset in me. It's the only game that forces the winner to announce that they are about to win before winning, so that everyone gets one last jab at him or her.

My parents had been preparing me all along to be mentally strong. Dad would create little signs around the court with positive affirmations written on them. Usually, our lessons would revolve around the mindful mantra of the day.

Mom would encourage us in other ways, mainly to visualize. Before Venus and I won any Grand Slams, we won them in our mind first, right there on our sidewalk.

Whatever you become, you become in your head first.

Welcome to the French Open, ladies and gentlemen.

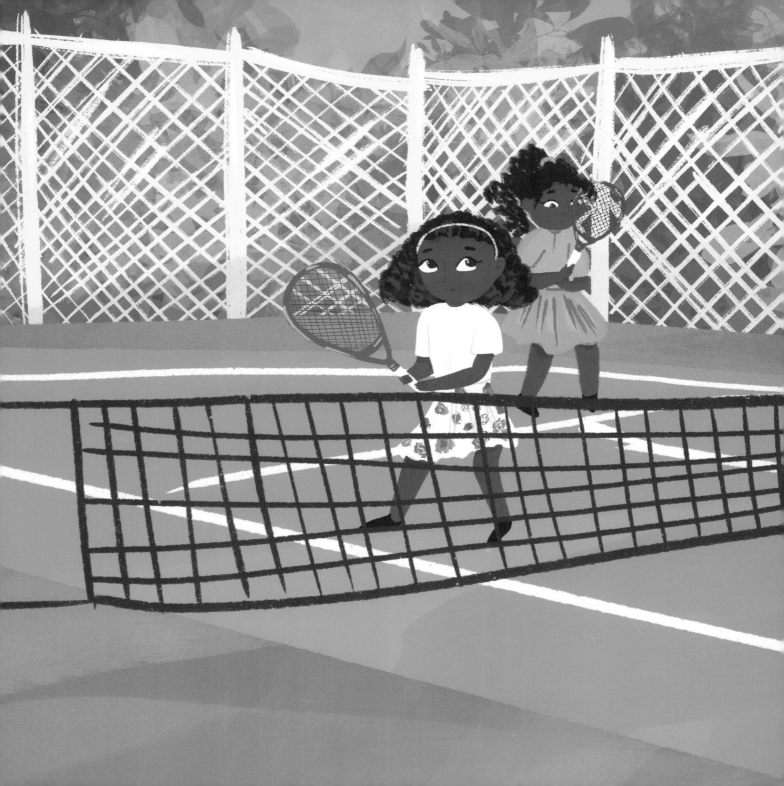

I didn't realize how much that mental strength would be needed as I grew up and we were teased about the color of our skin.

When I wasn't working on my mental game, I was working on my physical and technical game.

Dad would have me and Venus throw a football to each other before practicing our serves. It was a great way to get the snapping motion down.

10 and Under Tournament

When I was eight, I wanted to compete in tournaments so badly but my father wouldn't allow me to play. He wanted to wait until I was ready.

So I took matters into my own hands. When we arrived at one of Venus's tournaments, I walked up to the desk.

So there I was –
the youngest girl in
the draw competing
against girls older than me.

To my surprise and everyone else's, I made it to the finals. The only problem was that I had to play against my own sister.

I didn't know it at the time, but that was to be the first of many finals I would play against Venus. I was happy for my sister when she won, but I remember wishing it was me holding that gold trophy.

At fourteen years old, I made my debut as a professional. I lost a lot of matches at first, but that's pretty normal. Within two years, I became a top ten player. It wasn't easy, and it came with a lot of obstacles.

One of my hardest struggles was the discrimination I experienced in the sport I absolutely loved. On one occasion, people hurled racist comments at me and Venus.

During this time, I reached deep within to use the mental endurance my parents instilled in me. I kept a journal and wrote often in it. I turned to it when self doubt crept in, mostly between changeovers and matches. The positive affirmations strengthened my resolve and belief.

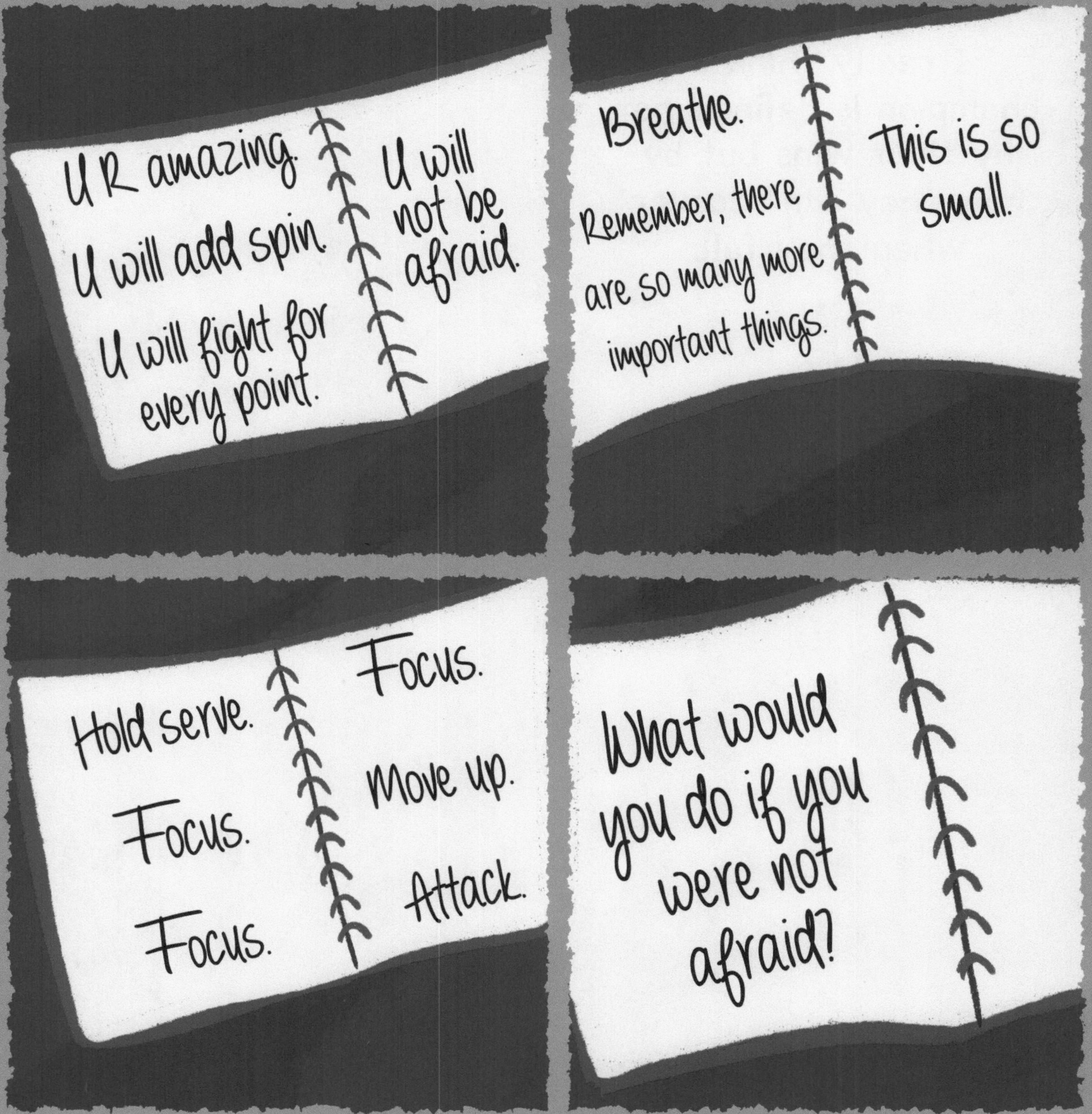
U R amazing.
U will add spin.
U will fight for every point.
U will not be afraid.
Breathe.
Remember, there are so many more important things.
This is so small.
Hold serve.
Focus.
Focus.
Focus.
Move up.
Attack.
What would you do if you were not afraid?

Becoming a champion is one part physical, one part technical, and many more parts mental.

Timeline

2001 – Serena experiences discrimination in professional tennis

2002 – Serena becomes the world number one for the first time in her career

2012 – Serena wins her fourth Olympic gold medal

2016 – Serena wins her 14th Doubles Grand Slam title

2017 – Serena becomes the only player, male or female, to win 10 plus grand slam singles titles in two separate decades; Wins her 23rd Singles Grand Slam title.

minimovers.tv

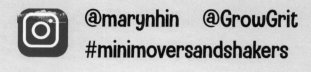

@marynhin   @GrowGrit
#minimoversandshakers

Mary Nhin   Grow Grit

Grow Grit

Printed in the USA
CPSIA information can be obtained
at www.ICGtesting.com
LVHW061920071223
765698LV00035B/8